Halford Mackinder
HEARTLAND

Halford Mackinder

HEARTLAND

Three Essays on Geopolitics

SPINEBILL PRESS

Spinebill Press
Katoomba NSW, Australia
spinebillpress.com

A catalogue record for this
book is available from the
National Library of Australia

ISBN 978-0-6485315-7-9

Design and typography by Michel Streich
Typeset in Caslon and Korolev Condensed

"Who rules East Europe commands the Heartland;
who rules the Heartland commands the World-Island;
who rules the World-Island controls the world."

HALFORD MACKINDER,
Democratic Ideals and Reality

ABOUT THE ESSAYS

The essays in this book represent important points in the development of Halford Mackinder's geopolitical theories.

The Geographical Pivot of History, published in 1904, is Mackinder's first presentation of his idea of the "Heartland", a concept he later expanded in his book *Democratic Ideals and Reality*. The essay *The Physical Basis of Political Geography*, published and presented in 1890 when Mackinder was in his late twenties and at the beginning of his academic career, is an early example of his novel approach to geography. In *The Round World and the Winning of the Peace*, written in 1943, less than five years before his death, Mackinder examines and adjusts his earlier heartland concept in the light of the changed political constellations during World War II.

CONTENTS

THE GEOGRAPHICAL
PIVOT OF HISTORY

WHEN HISTORIANS in the remote future come to look back on the group of centuries through which we are now passing, and see them foreshortened, as we today see the Egyptian dynasties, it may well be that they will describe the last 400 years as the Columbian epoch, and will say that it ended soon after the year 1900. Of late it has been a commonplace to speak of geographical exploration as nearly over, and it is recognised that geography must be diverted to the purpose of intensive survey and philosophic synthesis. In 400 years the outline of the map of the world has been completed with approximate accuracy, and even in the polar regions the voyages of Nansen and Scott have very narrowly reduced the last possibility of dramatic discoveries. But the opening of the twentieth century is appropriate as the end of a great historic epoch, not merely on account of this achievement, great though it be. The missionary, the conqueror, the farmer, the miner, and, of late, the engineer, have followed so closely in the traveller's footsteps that the world, in its remoter borders, has hardly been revealed before we must chronicle its virtually complete political appropriation.

In Europe, North America, South America, Africa, and Australasia there is scarcely a region left for the pegging out of a claim of ownership, unless as the result of a war between civilised or half-civilised powers. Even in Asia we are probably witnessing the last moves of the game first played by the horsemen of Yermak the Cossack and the shipmen of Vasco da Gama. Broadly speaking, we may contrast the Columbian epoch with the age which preceded it, by describing its essential characteristic as the expansion of Europe against almost negligible resistances, whereas mediaeval Christendom was pent into a narrow region and threatened by external barbarism. From the present time forth, in the post-Columbian age, we shall again have to deal with a closed political system, and none the less that it will be one of worldwide scope. Every explosion of social forces, instead of being dissipated in a surrounding circuit of unknown space and barbaric chaos, will be sharply re-echoed from the far side of the globe, and weak elements in the political and economic organism of the world will be shattered in consequence. There is a vast difference of effect in the fall of a shell into an earthwork and its fall amid the closed spaces and rigid structures of a great building or ship. Probably some half-consciousness of this fact is at last diverting much of the attention of statesmen in all parts of the world from territorial expansion to the struggle for relative efficiency.

It appears to me, therefore, that in the present decade we are for the first time in a position to attempt, with some degree of completeness, a correlation between the larger geographical and the larger historical generalisations. For the first time we can perceive something of the real proportion of features and events on the stage of the whole world, and may seek a formula which shall express certain aspects, at any rate, of geographical causation in universal history. If we are fortunate, that formula should have a practical value as setting into perspective some of the competing forces in current international politics. The familiar phrase about the westward march of empire is an empirical and fragmentary attempt of the kind. I propose this evening describing those physical features of the world which I believe to have been most coercive of human action, and presenting some of the chief phases of history as organically connected with them, even in the ages when they were unknown to geography. My aim will not be to discuss the influence of this or that kind of feature, or yet to make a study in regional geography, but rather to exhibit human history as part of the life of the world organism. I recognise that I can only arrive at one aspect of the truth, and I have no wish to stray into excessive materialism. Man and not nature initiates, but nature in large measure controls. My concern is with the general physical control, rather than the causes of universal history. It is obvious that only a first approximation to truth can be hoped for, I shall be humble to my critics.

The late Prof. Freeman held that the only history which counts is that of the Mediterranean and European races. In a sense, of course, this is true, for it is among these races that have originated the ideas which have rendered the inheritors of Greece and Rome dominant throughout the world. In another and very important sense, however, such a limitation has a cramping effect upon thought. The ideas which go to form a nation, as opposed to a mere crowd of human animals, have usually been accepted under the pressure of a common tribulation, and under a common necessity of resistance to external force. The idea of England was beaten into the Heptarchy by Danish and Norman conquerors; the idea of France was forced upon competing Franks, Goths, and Romans by the Huns at Chalons, and in the Hundred Years' War with England; the idea of

Christendom was born of the Roman persecutions, and matured by the Crusades; the idea of the United States was accepted, and local colonial patriotism sunk, only in the long War of Independence; the idea of the German Empire was reluctantly adopted in South Germany only after a struggle against France in comradeship with North Germany. What I may describe as the literary conception of history, by concentrating attention upon ideas and upon the civilisation which is their outcome, is apt to lose sight of the more elemental movements whose pressure is commonly the exciting cause of the efforts in which great ideas are nourished. A repellent personality performs a valuable social function in uniting his enemies, and it was under the pressure of external barbarism that Europe achieved her civilisation. I ask you, therefore, for a moment to look upon Europe and European history as subordinate to Asia and Asiatic history, for European civilisation is, in a very real sense, the outcome of the secular struggle against Asiatic invasion.

The most remarkable contrast in the political map of modern Europe is that presented by the vast area of Russia occupying half the Continent and the group of smaller territories tenanted by the Western Powers. From a physical point of view, there is, of course, a like contrast between the unbroken lowland of the east and the rich complex of mountains and valleys, islands and peninsulas, which together form the remainder of this part of the world. At first sight it would appear that in these familiar facts we have a correlation between natural environment and political organisation so obvious as hardly to be worthy of description, especially when we note that throughout the Russian plain a cold winter is opposed to a hot summer, and the conditions of human existence thus rendered additionally uniform. Yet a series of historical maps, such as that contained in the Oxford Atlas, will reveal the fact that not merely is the rough coincidence of European Russia with the Eastern Plain of Europe a matter of the last hundred years or so, but that in all earlier time there was persistent re-assertion of quite another tendency in the political grouping. Two groups of states usually divided the country into northern and southern political systems. The fact is that the orographical map does not express the particular physical contrast which has until very lately controlled human movement and settlement in Russia. When the screen of winter snow fades northward off the vast face of the plain, it is followed by rains whose maximum occurs in May and June beside the Black sea, but near the Baltic and White seas is deferred to July and August. In the south the later summer is a period of drought. As a consequence of this climatic regime, the north and north-west were forest broken only by marshes, whereas the south and south-east were a boundless grassy steppe, with trees only along the rivers. The line separating the two regions ran diagonally north-eastward from

EASTERN EUROPE BEFORE THE 19TH CENTURY

the northern end of the Carpathians to a point in the Ural range nearer to its southern than to its northern extremity. Moscow lies a little to north of this line, or, in other words, on the forest side of it. Outside Russia the boundary of the great forest ran westward almost exactly through the centre of the European isthmus, which is 800 miles across between the Baltic and the Black seas. Beyond this, in Peninsular Europe, the woods spread on through the plains of Germany in the north, while the steppe lands in the south turned the great Transylvanian bastion of the Carpathians, and extended up the Danube, through what are now the cornfields of Romania, to the Iron Gates. A detached area of steppes, known locally as Pusztas, now largely cultivated, occupied the plain of Hungary, ingirt by the forested rim of Carpathian and Alpine mountains. In all the west of Russia, save in the far north, the clearing of the forests, the drainage of the marshes, and the tillage of the steppes have recently averaged the character of the landscape, and in large measure obliterated a distinction which was formerly very coercive of humanity.

The earlier Russia and Poland were established wholly in the glades of the forest. Through the steppe on the other hand there came from the unknown

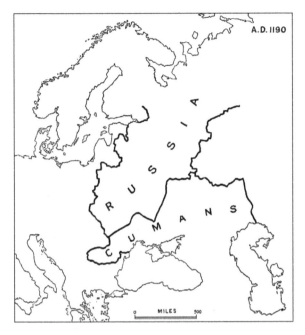

POLITICAL DIVISIONS OF EASTERN EUROPE
AT THE TIME OF THE 3RD CRUSADE

recesses of Asia, by the gateway between the Ural
mountains and the Caspian sea, in all the centuries
from the fifth to the sixteenth, a remarkable
succession of Turanian nomadic peoples – Huns,
Avars, Bulgarians, Magyars, Khazars, Patzinaks,
Cumans, Mongols, Kalmuks. Under Attila, the Huns
established themselves in the midst of the Pusztas,

in the uttermost Danubian outlier of the steppes, and thence dealt blows northward, westward, and south-ward against the settled peoples of Europe. A large part of modern history might be written as a commentary upon the changes directly or indirectly ensuing from these raids. The Angles and Saxons, it is quite possible, were then driven to cross the

POLITICAL DIVISIONS OF EASTERN EUROPE
AT THE ACCESSION OF CHARLES V

seas to found England in Britain. The Franks, the Goths, and the Roman provincials were compelled, for the first time, to stand shoulder to shoulder on the battlefield of Chalons, making common cause against the Asiatics, who were unconsciously welding together modern France. Venice was founded from the destruction of Aquileia and Padua; and even the Papacy owed a decisive prestige to the successful mediation of Pope Leo with Attila at Milan. Such was the harvest of results produced by a cloud of ruthless and idealess horsemen sweeping over the unimpeded plain – a blow, as it were, from the great Asiatic hammer striking freely through the vacant space. The Huns were followed by the Avars. It was for a marchland against these that Austria was founded, and Vienna fortified, as the result of the campaigns of Charlemagne. The Magyar came next, and by incessant raiding from his steppe base in Hungary increased the significance of the Austrian outpost, so drawing the political focus of Germany east-ward to the margin of the realm. The Bulgarian established a ruling caste south of the Danube, and has left his name upon the map, although his language has yielded to that of his Slavonic subjects. Perhaps the longest and most effective occupation of the Russian steppe proper was that of the Khazars, who were contemporaries of the great Saracen movement: the Arab geographers knew the Caspian as the Khazar sea. In the end, however, new hordes arrived from Mongolia, and for two centuries Russia in the northern forest was held tributary to the Mongol Khans of Kipchak, or "the Steppe", and Russian development was thus delayed and biassed at a time when the remainder of Europe was rapidly advancing.

It should be noted that the rivers running from the Forest to the Black and Caspian seas cross the whole breadth of the steppe-land path of the nomads, and that from time to time there were transient movements along their courses at right angles to the movement of the horsemen. Thus the missionaries of Greek Christianity ascended the Dnieper to Kiev, just as beforehand the Norse Varangians had descended the same river on their way to Constantinople. Still earlier, the Teutonic Goths appear for a moment upon the Dniester, having crossed Europe from the shores of the Baltic in the same south-eastward direction. But these are passing episodes which do not invalidate the broader generalisation. For a thousand years a series of horse-riding peoples emerged from Asia through the broad interval between the Ural mountains and the Caspian sea, rode through the open spaces of southern Russia, and struck home into Hungary in the very heart of the European peninsula, shaping by the necessity of opposing them the history of each of the great peoples around – the Russians, the Germans, the French, the Italians, and the Byzantine Greeks. That they stimulated healthy and powerful reaction, instead of crushing opposition under a widespread despotism, was due to the fact that the mobility of their power was conditioned by the steppes, and necessarily ceased in the surrounding forests and mountains.

A rival mobility of power was that of the Vikings in their boats. Descending from Scandinavia both upon the northern and the southern shores of Europe, they penetrated inland by the river ways. But the scope of their action was limited, for, broadly speaking, their power was effective only in the neighbourhood of the water. Thus the settled peoples of Europe lay gripped between two pressures – that of the Asiatic nomads from the east, and on the other three sides that of the pirates from the sea. From its very nature neither pressure was overwhelming, and both therefore were stimulative. It is noteworthy that the formative influence of the Scandinavians was second only in significance to that of the nomads, for under their attack both England and France made long moves towards unity, while the unity of Italy was broken by them. In earlier times, Rome had mobilised the power of her settled peoples by means of her roads, but the Roman roads had fallen into decay, and were not replaced until the eighteenth century.

It is likely that even the Hunnish invasion was by no means the first of the Asiatic series. The Scythians of the Homeric and Herodotian accounts, drinking the milk of mares, obviously practised the same arts of life, and were probably of the same race as the later inhabitants of the steppe. The Celtic element in the river names *Don*, *Do*wetz, *Dn*eiper, *Dn*eister, and *Dan*ube may possibly betoken the passage of peoples of similar habits, though not of identical race, but it is not unlikely that the Celts came merely from the northern forests, like the Goths and Varangians of a later time. The great wedge of population, however, which the anthropologists characterise as Brachy-Cephalic, driven westward from Brachy-Cephalic Asia through Central Europe into France, is apparently intrusive between the northern, western, and southern Dolico-Cephalic populations, and may very probably have been derived from Asia.[1]

The full meaning of Asiatic influence upon Europe is not, however, discernible until we come to the Mongol invasions of the fifteenth century; but before we analyze the essential facts concerning these, it is desirable to shift our geographical viewpoint from Europe, so that we may consider the Old World in its entirety. It is obvious that, since the rainfall is derived from the sea, the heart of the greatest land mass is likely to be relatively dry. We are not, therefore, surprised to find that two thirds of all the world's population is concentrated in relatively small areas along the margins of the great continent – in Europe, beside the Atlantic ocean; in the Indies and China, beside the Indian and Pacific oceans. A vast belt of almost uninhabited, because practically rainless, land extends as the Sahara completely across Northern Africa into Arabia. Central and Southern Africa were almost as completely severed from Europe and Asia throughout the greater part of history as were the Americas and Australia. In fact, the southern boundary of Europe was and is the Sahara rather than the Mediterranean, for it is the desert which divides the black man from the white. The continuous land-mass of Euro-Asia thus included between the ocean and the desert measures 21,000,000 square miles, or half of all the land on the globe, if we exclude from reckoning the deserts of Sahara and

27

Arabia. There are many detached deserts scattered through Asia, from Syria and Persia north-eastward to Manchuria, but no such continuous vacancy as to be comparable with the Sahara. On the other hand, Euro-Asia is characterised by a very remarkable distribution of river drainage. Throughout an immense portion of the centre and north, the rivers have been practically useless for purposes of human communication with the outer world. The Volga, the Oxus, and the Jaxartes drain into salt lakes; the Obi, the Yenisei, and the Lena into the frozen ocean of the north. These are six of the greatest rivers in the world. There are many smaller but still considerable streams in the same area, such as the Tarim and the Helmund, which similarly fail to reach the ocean. Thus the core of Euro-Asia, although mottled with desert patches, is on the whole a steppe-land supplying a wide-spread if often scanty pasture, and there are not a few river-fed oases in it, but it is wholly unpenetrated by waterways from the ocean. In other words, we have in this immense area all the conditions for the maintenance of a sparse, but in the aggregate considerable, population of horse-riding and camel-riding nomads. Their realm is limited northward by a broad belt of sub-arctic forest and marsh, wherein the climate is too rigorous, except

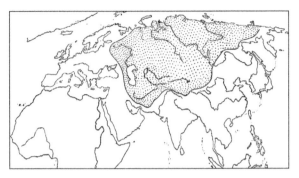

CONTINENTAL AND ARCTIC DRAINAGE
Equal area projection

at the eastern and western extremities, for the
development of agricultural settlements. In the east
the forests extend southward to the Pacific coast in
the Amur land and Manchuria. Similarly in the west,
in prehistoric Europe, forest was the predominant
vegetation. Thus framed in to the north-east, north,
and north-west, the steppes spread continuously
for 4,000 miles from the Pusztas of Hungary to
the Little Gobi of Manchuria, and, except in their
westernmost extremity, they are untraversed by
rivers draining to an accessible ocean, for we may
neglect the very recent efforts to trade to the mouths
of the Obi and Yenisei. In Europe, Western Siberia,
and Western Turkestan the steppe lands lie low, in

some places below the level of the sea. Further to east, in Mongolia, they extend over plateaux; but the passage from the one level to the other, over the naked, unscarped lower ranges of the arid heartland, presents little difficulty.

The hordes which ultimately fell upon Europe in the middle of the fourteenth century gathered their first force 3,000 miles away on the high steppes of Mongolia. The havoc wrought for a few years in Poland, Silesia, Moravia, Hungary, Croatia, and Serbia was, however, but the remotest and the most transient result of the great stirring of the nomads of the East associated with the name of Ghenghis Khan. While the Golden Horde occupied the steppe of Kipchak, from the Sea of Aral, through the interval between the Ural range and the Caspian, to the foot of the Carpathians, another horde, descending south-westward between the Caspian sea and the Hindu Kush into Persia, Mesopotamia, and even into Syria, founded the domain of the Ilkhan. A third subsequently struck into Northern China, conquering Cathay. India and Mangi, or Southern China, were for a time sheltered by the incomparable barrier of Tibet, to whose efficacy there is, perhaps, nothing similar in the world, unless it be the Sahara desert and the polar ice. But at a later time, in the days of Marco Polo in the case of Mangi, in those of Tamerlane in the case of India, the obstacle was circumvented. Thus it happened that in this typical and well-recorded instance, all the settled margins of the Old World sooner or later felt the expansive force of mobile power originating in the steppe. Russia, Persia, India, and China were either made tributary, or received Mongol dynasties. Even the incipient power of the Turks in Asia Minor was struck down for half a century.

As in the case of Europe, so in other marginal lands of Euro-Asia there are records of earlier invasions. China had more than once to submit to conquest from the north; India several times to conquest from the north-west. In the case of Persia, however, at least one of the earlier descents has a special significance in the history of Western civilisation. Three or four centuries before the Mongols, the Seljuk Turks, emerging from Central Asia, overran by this path an immense area of the land, which we may describe as of the five seas – Caspian, Black, Mediterranean, Ked, and Persian. They established themselves at Kerman, at Hamadan, and in Asia Minor, and they overthrew the Saracen dominion of Baghdad and Damascus. It was ostensibly to punish their treatment of the Christian pilgrims at Jerusalem that Christendom undertook the great series of campaigns known collectively as the Crusades. Although these failed in their immediate objects, they so stirred and united Europe that we may count them as the beginning of modern history – another striking instance of European advance stimulated by the necessity of reacting against pressure from the heart of Asia.

The conception of Euro-Asia to which we thus attain is that of a continuous land, ice-girt in the north, water-girt elsewhere, measuring 21 million square miles, or more than three times the area of North America, whose centre and north, measuring some 9 million square miles, or more than twice the area of Europe, have no available waterways to the ocean, but, on the other hand, except in the sub-arctic forest, are very generally favourable to the mobility of horsemen and camelmen. To east, south, and west of this heart-land are marginal regions, ranged in a vast crescent, accessible to shipmen. According to physical conformation, these regions are four in number, and it is not a little remarkable that in a general way they respectively coincide with the spheres of the four great religions – Buddhism, Brahminism, Mahometanism, and Christianity. The first two are the monsoon lands, turned the one towards the Pacific, and the other towards the

Indian ocean. The fourth is Europe, watered by the Atlantic rains from the west. These three together, measuring less than 7 million square miles, have more than 1,000 million people, or two thirds of the world population. The third, coinciding with the land of the Five Seas, or, as it is more often described, the Nearer East, is in large measure deprived of moisture by the proximity of Africa, and, except in the oases, is therefore thinly peopled. In some degree it partakes of the characteristics both of the marginal belt and of the central area of Euro-Asia. It is mainly devoid of forest, is patched with desert, and is therefore suitable for the operations of the nomad. Dominantly, however, it is marginal, for sea-gulfs and oceanic rivers lay it open to sea power, and permit of the exercise of such power from it. As a consequence, periodically throughout history, we have here had empires belonging essentially to the marginal series, based on the agricultural populations of the great oases of Babylonia and Egypt, and in free water-communication with the civilised worlds of the Mediterranean and the Indies. But, as we should expect, these empires have been subject to an unparalleled series of revolutions, some due to Scythian, Turkish, and Mongol raids from Central Asia, others to the effort of the Mediterranean peoples to conquer the overland ways from the western to the eastern ocean. Here is the weakest spot in the girdle of early civilisations, for the isthmus of Suez divided sea-power into Eastern and Western, and the arid wastes of Persia advancing from Central Asia to the Persian gulf gave constant opportunity for nomad-power to strike home to the ocean edge, dividing India and China, on the one hand, from the Mediterranean world on the other. Whenever the Babylonian, the Syrian, and the Egyptian oases were weakly held, the steppe-peoples could treat the open tablelands of Iran and Asia Minor as forward posts whence to strike through the Punjab into India, through Syria into Egypt, and over the broken bridge of the Bosphorus and Dardanelles into Hungary. Vienna stood in the gateway of Inner Europe, withstanding the nomadic raids, both those which came by the direct road through the Russian steppe, and those which came by the loop way to south of the Black and Caspian seas.

Here we have illustrated the essential difference between the Saracen and the Turkish controls of the Nearer East. The Saracens were a branch of the Semitic race, essentially peoples of the Euphrates and Nile and of the smaller oases of Lower Asia. They created a great empire by availing themselves of the two mobilities permitted by their land – that of the horse and camel on the one hand, that of the ship on the other. At different times their fleets controlled both the Mediterranean as far as Spain, and the Indian ocean to the Malay islands. From their strategically central position between the eastern and western oceans, they attempted the conquest of all the marginal lands of the Old World, imitating Alexander and anticipating Napoleon. They could even threaten the steppe land. Wholly distinct from Arabia as from Europe, India, and China were the Turanian pagans from the closed heart of Asia, the Turks who destroyed the Saracen civilisation.

Mobility upon the ocean is the natural rival of horse and camel mobility in the heart of the continent. It was upon navigation of oceanic rivers that was based the Potamic stage of civilisation, that of China on the Yangtze, that of India on the Ganges, that of Babylonia on the Euphrates, that of Egypt on the Nile. It was essentially upon the navigation of the Mediterranean that was based what has been described as the Thalassic stage of civilisation, that of the Greeks and Romans. The Saracens and the Vikings held sway by navigation of the oceanic coasts.

The all-important result of the discovery of the

Cape road to the Indies was to connect the western and eastern coastal navigations of Euro-Asia, even though by a circuitous route, and thus in some measure to neutralise the strategical advantage of the central position of the steppe-nomads by pressing upon them in rear. The revolution commenced by the great mariners of the Columbian generation endowed Christendom with the widest possible mobility of power, short of a winged mobility. The one and continuous ocean enveloping the divided and insular lands is, of course, the geographical condition of ultimate unity in the command of the sea, and of the whole theory of modern naval strategy and policy as expounded by such writers as Captain Mahan and Mr. Spencer Wilkinson. The broad political effect was to reverse the relations of Europe and Asia, for whereas in the Middle Ages Europe was caged between an impassable desert to south, an unknown ocean to west, and icy or forested wastes to north and north-east, and in the east and south-east was constantly threatened by the superior mobility of the horsemen and camelmen, she now emerged upon the world, multiplying more than thirty-fold the sea surface and coastal lands to which she had access, and wrapping her influence round the Euro-Asiatic land-power which had hitherto threatened her very existence. New Europes were created in the vacant lands discovered in the midst of the waters, and what Britain and Scandinavia were to Europe in the earlier time, that have America and Australia, and in some measure even Trans-Saharan Africa, now become to Euro-Asia. Britain, Canada, the United States, South Africa, Australia, and Japan are now a ring of outer and insular bases for sea-power and commerce, inaccessible to the land-power of Euro-Asia.

But the land power still remains, and recent events have again increased its significance. While the maritime peoples of Western Europe have covered the ocean with their fleets, settled the outer continents, and in varying degree made tributary the oceanic margins of Asia, Russia has organised the Cossacks, and, emerging from her northern forests, has policed the steppe by setting her own nomads to meet the Tartar nomads. The Tudor century, which saw the expansion of Western Europe over the sea, also saw Russian power carried from Moscow through Siberia. The eastward swoop of the horsemen across Asia was an event almost as pregnant with political consequences as was the rounding of the Cape, although the two movements long remained apart.

It is probably one of the most striking co-incidences of history that the seaward and the landward expansion of Europe should, in a sense, continue the ancient opposition between Roman and Greek. Few great failures have had more far-reaching consequences than the failure of Rome to Latinise the Greek. The Teuton was civilised and Christianised by the Roman, the Slav in the main by the Greek. It is the Romano-Teuton who in later times embarked upon the ocean; it was the Graeco-Slav who rode over the steppes, conquering the Turanian. Thus the modern land-power differs from the sea-power no less in the source of its ideals than in the material conditions of its mobility.[2]

In the wake of the Cossack, Russia has safely emerged from her former seclusion in the northern forests. Perhaps the change of greatest intrinsic importance which took place in Europe in the last century was the southward migration of the Russian peasants, so that, whereas agricultural settlements formerly ended at the forest boundary, the centre of the population of all European Russia now lies to south of that boundary, in the midst of the wheat-fields which have replaced the more western steppes. Odessa has here risen to importance with the rapidity of an American city.

A generation ago steam and the Suez canal appeared to have increased the mobility of sea-power relatively to land-power. Railways acted chiefly as feeders to ocean-going commerce. But trans-continental railways are now transmuting the conditions of land-power, and nowhere can they have such effect as in the closed heartland of Euro-Asia, in vast areas of which neither timber nor accessible stone was available for road-making. Railways work the greater wonders in the steppe, because they directly replace horse and camel mobility, the road stage of development having here been omitted.

In the matter of commerce it must not be forgotten that ocean-going traffic, however relatively cheap, usually involves the fourfold handling of goods – at the factory of origin, at the export wharf, at the import wharf, and at the inland warehouse for retail distribution; whereas the continental railway truck may run direct from the exporting factory into the importing warehouse. Thus marginal ocean-fed commerce tends, other things being equal, to form a zone of penetration round the continents, whose inner limit is roughly marked by the line along which the cost of four handlings, the oceanic freight, and the railway freight from the neighbouring coast, is equivalent to the cost of two handlings and the

NATURAL SEATS OF POWER (*rotate image*)
Pivot area – wholly continental; *Outer crescent* – wholly
oceanic; *Inner crescent* – partly continental, partly oceanic

continental railway freight. English and German coals are said to compete on such terms midway through Lombardy.

The Russian railways have a clear run of 6,000 miles from Wirballen in the west to Vladivostok in the east. The Russian army in Manchuria is as significant evidence of mobile land-power as the British army in South Africa was of sea-power. True, that the Trans-Siberian railway is still a single and precarious line of communication, but the century will not be old before all Asia is covered with railways.

The spaces within the Russian Empire and Mongolia are so vast, and their potentialities in population, wheat, cotton, fuel, and metals so incalculably great, that it is inevitable that a vast economic world, more or less apart, will there develop inaccessible to oceanic commerce.

As we consider this rapid review of the broader currents of history, does not a certain persistence of geographical relationship become evident? Is not the pivot region of the world's politics that vast area of Euro-Asia which is inaccessible to ships, but in antiquity lay open to the horse-riding nomads, and is today about to be covered with a network of railways? There have been and are here the conditions of a mobility of military and economic power of a far-reaching and yet limited character. Russia replaces the Mongol Empire. Her pressure on Finland, on Scandinavia, on Poland, on Turkey, on Persia, on India, and on China, replaces the centrifugal raids of the steppemen. In the world at large she occupies the central strategical position held by Germany in Europe. She can strike on all sides and be struck from all sides, save the north. The full development of her modern railway mobility is merely a matter of time. Nor is it likely that any possible social revolution will alter her essential relations to the great geographical limits of her existence. Wisely recognising the fundamental limits of her power, her rulers have parted with Alaska; for it is as much a law of policy for Russia to own nothing over seas as for Britain to be supreme on the ocean.

Outside the pivot area, in a great inner crescent, are Germany, Austria, Turkey, India, and China, and in an outer crescent, Britain, South Africa, Australia, the United States, Canada, and Japan. In the present condition of the balance of power, the pivot state, Russia, is not equivalent to the peripheral states, and there is room for an equipoise in France. The United States has recently become an eastern power, affecting the European balance not directly, but through Russia, and she will construct the Panama canal to make her Mississippi and Atlantic resources available in the Pacific. From this point of view the real divide between east and west is to be found in the Atlantic ocean.

The oversetting of the balance of power in favour of the pivot state, resulting in its expansion over the marginal lands of Euro-Asia, would permit of the use of vast continental resources for fleet-building, and the empire of the world would then be in sight. This might happen if Germany were to ally herself with Russia. The threat of such an event should, therefore, throw France into alliance with the over-sea powers, and France, Italy, Egypt, India, and Korea would become so many bridge heads where the outside navies would support armies to compel the pivot allies to deploy land forces and prevent them from concentrating their whole strength on fleets. On a smaller scale that was what Wellington accomplished from his sea-base at Torres Vedras in the Peninsular War. May not this in the end prove to be the strategical function of India in the British Imperial system? Is not this the idea underlying Mr. Amery's conception that the British military front stretches from the Cape through India to Japan?

The development of the vast potentialities of

South America might have a decisive influence upon the system. They might strengthen the United States, or, on the other hand, if Germany were to challenge the Monroe Doctrine successfully, they might detach Berlin from what I may perhaps describe as a pivot policy. The particular combinations of power brought into balance are not material; my contention is that from a geographical point of view they are likely to rotate round the pivot state, which is always likely to be great, but with limited mobility as compared with the surrounding marginal and insular powers.

I have spoken as a geographer. The actual balance of political power at any given time is, of course, the product, on the one hand, of geographical conditions, both economic and strategic, and, on the other hand, of the relative number, virility, equipment, and organisation of the competing peoples. In proportion as these quantities are accurately estimated are we likely to adjust differences without the crude resort to arms. And the geographical quantities in the calculation are more measurable and more nearly constant than the human. Hence we should expect to find our formula apply equally to past history and to present politics. The social movements of all times have played around essentially the game physical features, for I doubt whether the progressive desiccation of Asia and Africa, even if proved, has in historical times vitally altered the human environment. The westward march of empire appears to me to have been a short rotation of marginal power round the south-western and western edge of the pivotal area. The Nearer, Middle, and Far Eastern questions relate to the unstable equilibrium of inner and outer powers in those parts of the marginal crescent where local power is, at present, more or less negligible.

In conclusion, it may be well expressly to point out that the substitution of some new control of the inland area for that of Russia would not tend to reduce the geographical significance of the pivot position.

Were the Chinese, for instance, organised by the Japanese, to overthrow the Russian Empire and conquer its territory, they might constitute the yellow peril to the world's freedom just because they would add an oceanic frontage to the resources of the great continent, an advantage as yet denied to the Russian tenant of the pivot region.

THE PHYSICAL BASIS
OF POLITICAL GEOGRAPHY

MY SUBJECT THIS EVENING IS a large one. Taken in its widest meaning, the title of my paper seems to invite you to a philosophical discussion on the Free-will question. It is not, however, my intention either to attack, to defend, or to illustrate Buckle's *History of Civilisation*. Suffice it for my purpose that both parties of historians – those who regard man's initiative and those who regard his environment as the more important – both allow at least a large influence in the shaping of his history to the particular stages on which nations play their parts. It is my object this evening to state a few of the ways in which geographical features govern or, at least, guide history, and to give a few of the examples on which my principles are based.

The chief distinction in political geography seems to be founded on the facts that man travels and man settles. Nature has very different relations to travelling and to settling man. Travelling man seeks lines of least resistance over the opposing world. Settling man studies chiefly productivity and security of tenure. A chain of oases in a desert, a fertile valley in a mountain system, may be able to support very few settlers, and yet be a great highway along which emigrants, armies, and merchants have thronged since prehistoric ages. Consider the great barrier of the Alps – no mere boundary wall of Italy, but a whole natural region – a rugged *belt* on the map of Europe, as large as the British Isles, yet so unsuited for settlement that it contains a population not twice as large as that of London. Consider, on the other hand, the passes through those same Alps – all the historic goings to and fro which they have permitted: Gauls swarming to the loot of Italy; legions tramping to the conquest of Gaul and Vindelicia; German hordes bettering the lessons Rome had taught them, descending, half to spoil, half to ennoble the civilisation they took over from antiquity; pilgrims from the extremities to the heart of Christendom; emperors progressing from the German to the Italian half of their Holy Roman Empire; the riches of the East borne from Venice to Augsburg; Suvaroff; Bonaparte; the modern locomotive – all threading narrow valley bottoms – valleys studded with slender strings of village spires, and shut in on either hand by walls and wastes of rock and snow. Set in contrast to the Alps the great plain of Ireland, teeming with population even today, fifty years ago with as many souls as now inhabit the four-times larger Alps; yet, Ireland at the ends of the world, on the road to nowhere, and with a history which rarely touches even the skirts of European politics. The key to the political geography of the Alps is that they are a barrier with definite, though many gates, separating two great unlike areas of settlement. The key to the political geography of Ireland is that it is an area of settlement, productive and relatively free from internal barriers, but possessing not a single line of communication important to the outer world.

In each of these relations there are two things related; Man travelling or settling, and Nature, and each member of the couples is variable. History is the record of part of Man's variation, Geology that of part of Nature's. Yet for the purposes of political geography Nature may be regarded as invariable, when compared, that is, with the short kaleidoscopic evolution of human arts.[3] Thus the resistance offered by a given feature to man's movement, or the facilities of a given area for his settlement, are forever varying with the state of his civilisation. In applying geography to the lighting up of history, the physical features may, as a first approximation, be treated as constant, rock-like; around them the human flood surges and rests, ebbs and flows – now calmly contained in its basin, now sweeping over, bursting through, or wearing away the obstacles. We can imagine a time, though we do not know of it, before paddles, before oars, before sails, when all movement was on land and the sea an absolute barrier. Then came an age of coasting, when the high seas, however, still defied the ancients, though not because of their glue-like consistency as the impotent mariners would have it. With the compass the resistance of the ocean fell, and it continued to fall until, at the beginning of this century, all the shipping arts combined to give water so trifling a resistance as compared with rock that men took it inland in canals. Then suddenly George Stephenson almost reversed in this respect the whole current of history. The resistance of water continued to fall, it is true, but that of land fell so out of all proportion that it is now lower than that of water. Where men used to come from the East up the Adriatic to Venice, they now pass to Brindisi, and by land up the long peninsula of Italy. They will soon go from London to India by land; they have gone recently all the way by ocean. Thus, while the mountains change their form almost imperceptibly in long ages, a daring leader, a mechanical discovery, a great engineering monument, may revolutionise man's relations to geography in the third of a generation. The suddenness with which the results of these revolutions become apparent is far more marked as a rule in the case of man travelling than man settling. Roads, even main roads, are far more easily abandoned than settlements. Once on the move, we have but to swerve from the beaten track to accomplish the change: there is some resistance even to this, but nothing to be compared to the inertia with which men cling to old settlements. Witness the beggar population of decayed cities. Love of home, love of family, want of imagination, want of knowledge, want of means, want of energy, combine to keep men stationary. To human inertia must be added, in modern days especially, the inertia of capital. Even if we grant that with present conditions Milford Haven is a better terminus to the transatlantic ferry than Liverpool, the fixed capital of Liverpool would impede change until, with the change of conditions, the advantages of Milford Haven became overwhelming. So, too, it may be that the balance of geographical advantages has already inclined against England, and that she is maintaining her position by inertia – by the difficulty attending the removal of the men, the capital, the skill, and the traditions accumulated here as the result of past geographical advantages. We may sum up this stage of our discussion by saying that while political geography investigates the relations between Nature and Man, travelling or settling, that while man's modes of travelling and settling vary often suddenly, and therefore his relations to Nature vary as suddenly, yet these changed relations do not always find immediate geographical expression owing to what we may call geographical inertia, the tendency of settlements and the less tendency of roads to remain fixed.[4]

A distinction, however, must be drawn among settlements. Paradoxical as it may seem, some settlements are more dependent on movement than on settlement. This is notably the case with some of the concentrated settlements known as towns. The point is easiest shown by a pair of examples. Ireland is a productive pastoral land, with a fairly dense population evenly distributed over its surface, with a great number of villages and small country towns, but with no great centres of population, except at half-a-dozen ports, where men and goods converge to enter and to leave the island. This is a true area of settlement based on the productivity of the land and independent of roads. Southern Bavaria, on the other hand, is a relatively barren inhospitable upland with a sparse population, and yet it contains at least four great historic cities, Ratisbon, Munich, Augsburg, and Ulm. Great and important today – in the past still greater – these cities have not grown rich on Bavarian produce. They are nodal points on through lines of traffic from the north to the south, from the east to the west of Europe. The expression "nodal point" is a convenient one. A nodal point occurs wherever there is a congestion of traffic on a road, at a ferry or a bridge, at the mouth of a gorge, where two roads cross or join, at a changing place of vehicles whether from pack-horse to ship, railway-truck to steamer, or river-barge to sea-going vessel. Wherever, in fact, traffic is delayed or is swollen, there is the proper spot for all the trades that wait on the traffic to fix their abode, the publican and the shoeing-smith at the four ways in the country, the merchant and the docket at the place of transhipment or assortment. This does not pretend to be exhaustive of the causes of towns. It is only true of a great number of towns that they are incident to man's travelling. Others are the market centres or administrative centres of productive areas, the results of the settlement of socially organised man.

The distinction between man travelling and man settling must not be treated in a narrow spirit. It is not intended as a tool for the rote-workman.

In all but the most elementary organisations of society travelling and settling are intricately related. The precise value of the contrast as a method of geographical analysis will be best gathered from examples. I have time only for one, but that on the greatest scale.

If we look at a physical map of the Old World, we shall notice that the greatest land mass is crossed in different directions by a belt of inland seas and a belt of deserts. If we further consider a map of the same region on which the density of population is indicated approximately by depth of tinting, we shall have our attention drawn to the fact that there are two great regions densely populated, Europe and South-Eastern Asia. We are to deal with the relations of these three phenomena. The belt of deserts lies between the two deeply tinted populated areas, separating them. The belt of seas – the Mediterranean and the Red Seas – crosses the desert belt diagonally, and, were it not for the Isthmus of Suez, would form a water road connecting by almost the shortest line the two populated areas. Let us now make a closer examination of each of the three features. First the settlements. The western (European) area may perhaps be spoken of physically as the Gulf-stream region – that is a district blown over by prevalent west winds fed with warmth and moisture from the warm surface waters of the Atlantic. It is largely this influence which has made so northern a region so highly favourable to settlement. Historically this is the Roman world. Its morals, its law, its religion, its traditions, much even of its languages, are legacies from Rome. Its states, though independent, form a system held together mainly by the common Roman factor. Physically and historically, then, we are dealing with one great area of settlement. Its boundaries are not, however, quite coincident with those of Europe, for Barbary must be included in it, and all but South-western Russia must be excluded. The inclusion and the exclusion are on physical and historical grounds which are obvious. This Gulf-stream Roman area of settlement has 300 million inhabitants.

The South eastern Asiatic area is suited to settlement because moist and hot, because therefore rich in vegetable products. The moisture is brought by the monsoons from the tropical ocean. Hence physically it may be known as the Monsoon-area. Politically its unity, though not so marked as the Roman unity, will perhaps justify the expression Indo-Chinese. It extends from India to Japan. It has 700 million inhabitants.

Thus these two areas contain together 1,000 million people, two-thirds of the world's population. The products of the two regions are as different as their climates. The civilisations of the two communities differ in every detail. The differences are a measure of the number of new commodities, new ideas, even new men, which one has to offer to the other. The vastness of the populations is a measure of the demand for the commodities, ideas, and men, once the supply is made known. Both together, difference of products and vastness of populations, measure the necessity of communication between the two areas of settlement. History is to a great extent one long comment on the importance of the East and West trade.

Now turn to the facilities for travel from the one area to the other. The two are held apart by the great desert belt. Indeed they are two, not one, *because* of this belt. True, the desert contains small areas fit for settlement – oases, river-valleys, "curtains" of mountain chains – but as a whole it is not an area for settlement. It is a barrier of very high resistance even to travelling man. It extends as the Sahara from the very shore line of the Atlantic until it ends as the Gobi, almost on the confines of Siberia. In the west it is a more effective barrier than the sea itself.

Despite the Mediterranean, Barbary is European in flora, fauna, men and history, not a member of Negroland. The lines of least resistance through these deserts must clearly be geographical features of first-rate importance. Were it only complete, the belt of seas which we have mentioned crossing the desert belt would rob the deserts of half their severing power. Actually the communication is broken by the Isthmus of Suez. All history would have been radically different but for Suez. It is the most important spot on the face of the earth. It owes its power, however, not merely to its land-character, but to the north wind which blows persistently down two-thirds of the Red Sea, and which almost defies the mariner to make the passage up the sea. It required the modern combination of canal and steam definitely to reduce the obstruction.

The sea road was, then, for long ages, largely closed. So much the more important the remaining lines of low resistance. They are few, definite, and of two types – either rivers struggling through the deserts from well-watered source-lands, or else what Orientals term "curtains of the mountains" strips of green country at the mountain foot and parallel with the range, nourished by the moisture which in these lands only mountain-crests can wring from the winds. Of the former class we have the Nile, the Euphrates and Tigris, the Oxus and Jaxartes. Of the latter we have chiefly the roads which follow the Arabian mountains near the Red Sea shore and those which accompany the northern and southern Persian ranges.

The men who dwelt on the oasis-roads from east to west formed naturally the first commercial peoples. Babylonians, Phoenicians, Jews, Arabs – they were chiefly of one race; and may we not trace the hereditary commercial aptitudes of that great Semitic race to the necessities and opportunities of their remarkable position? While the peoples of the oases took a toll of the East and West traffic, and hence were some of the first to grow rich and civilised, their existence had another curious effect on the world's history. They drew a veil between East and West which heightened the effect of the desert. To borrow a simile from physics, this veil was transparent to things, but not to ideas. Silk passed from Chinese hands to Desert hands, and from Desert hands to Roman hands but all that Greeks and Romans knew of China was summed up in its name, Serica, the silk land, and that a name unknown in China. It was because the West nowhere touched the East, because Western knowledge of the East was only hearsay, because the West in a word looked at the East through a glass darkly, that old writers could place in the Indies what were in effect the fairy tales of the Middle Ages. Such rays of coloured light as now and then struggled through only served to stimulate imagination. We moderns have discovered the world, but we have lost the geographical stage of romance. We cannot yet measure the loss. What a part these Desert, or better, Oasis peoples have played in the world's history! What do we not owe to them directly or indirectly in commerce, science, art, romance? Do not the characteristics of their homes throw a flood of light on their nature and development?

It was the overthrow of the oasis civilisations by the Turks which precipitated the greatest revolution in history. The Turks were to the Desert what the Teutons were to the West. In each case a barbaric flood overwhelmed an ancient civilisation, the toil-some growth of ages. But while the Teutons came down on one end of the inhabited world, leaving it free to be slowly penetrated again by Byzantine and Saracen light, the Turks broke the slender links between East and West. They broke them, too, just when they had become indispensable to the West. The Crusades had made Eastern luxuries necessities to reborn Europe. The West, full of the energy of new youth, fired by recovered knowledge and recovered religion, set itself to find new roads to the Indies – ocean roads, not desert roads. Columbus sought the Indies by the west, Magellan by the south-west, Da Gama by the south-east, Cabot and Davis by the north-west, Barentz and Chancellor by the north-east, Henry Hudson by the north over the North Pole. In thirty years the broad features of the world were revealed. Ever since, geographically, politically too, we have but filled in what that great age sketched out.

Are we not justified, then, in saying that the greatest events in the world's history, ancient, medieval, and modern, are at least related to the greatest features of geography? The twin character of the world's civilisation, Roman and Indo-Chinese, is based on the two areas for settlement severed by the vacant desert. The narrow paths through the waste, the same in all ages, are the homes of the oasis peoples, small in number when compared with eastern and western hundreds of millions, yet at once the intermediaries and the obstructives between East and West. Here is the grandest contrast between man settling and man travelling, between true settlements and settlements chiefly ancillary to travel.

My time is up. I might give many more examples. That which I have given is a large one, implying the knowledge of few details of physical geography. It may, however, I trust, suffice to show that there are higher flights for the political geographer than the mere mapping of frontiers and detailing of statistics. Humdrum detail is the greater part of every science, but no science can satisfy the mind which does not allow of the building of palaces out of its bricks. In this sense it is often said that the physical geographer and the historian may exist, but not the political geographer. Yet I venture to say that his (the political geographer's) is the crowning chapter of geography. He requires physical geography as a preliminary – what the Germans call a *Hilfswissenschaft*, we more clumsily an auxiliary science. He takes a different view of history from that of the historian proper. The latter has not time or, as a rule, aptitude to gain the necessary steeping in physical geography. Political geography has in this sense a distinct service to render both to history and to politics. Cannot the "must be" suggest a solution of the "has been"? John Richard Green showed us how to use this implement where other evidence is wanting or weak. Even where evidence of events is strong, evidence of causes is often weak. Even where all is clear – and how rare this – causes and effects, some of the causes must be intricately geographical. And in politics, how small does current diplomacy seem, if we realise to the full how deep are the ruts in which a nation's course is run. The course of politics is the product of two sets of forces, impelling and guiding. The impetus is from the past, is the history imbedded in a people's character and traditions. The present guides the movement by economic wants and geographical opportunities. Statesmen and diplomatists succeed and fail pretty much as they recognise the irresistible power of these forces. This analysis is our only key to the future. In an age when democracy has ultimately to guide policy – though, busy earning its living, it has no time and little opportunity to study current diplomacy – broad principles can alone keep it right. The geographer has to help in stating these principles. The task is a vast one: perhaps to those absorbed in the close study of details even a distasteful one, certainly one bound to lead to falls, to lead to truth only through repeated error. This is a great ideal, some will think too great, but there is room for all. We may stop short in the reasoning at whatever stage we, each of us, will. Our highest ideal is attainable only to future generations, and none the worse for that.

THE ROUND WORLD AND
THE WINNING OF THE PEACE

I HAVE BEEN ASKED to carry further some of the themes with which I have dealt in my past writings, in particular to consider whether my strategical concept of a "Heartland" has lost any of its significance under the conditions of modern warfare. In order to set the concept into its context, I must begin with a short account of how it originally came to take shape.

My earliest memory of public affairs goes back to the day in September 1870 when, as a small boy who had just begun attendance at the local grammar school, I took home the news, which I had learned from a telegram affixed to the post office door, that Napoleon III and his whole army had surrendered to the Prussians at Sedan. This came as a shock to Englishmen, who still moved mentally in the wake of Trafalgar and the retreat from Moscow, but the full effect of it was not realised until some years later. Britain's supremacy on the ocean had not yet been challenged, and the only danger she saw at that time to her overseas empire was in the Asiatic position of Russia. During this period the London newspapers were quick to detect evidence of Russian intrigue in every rumour from Constantinople and in every tribal disturbance along the northwest frontier of India. British sea power and Russian land power held the center of the international stage.

Thirty years later, at the turn of the century, von Tirpitz began to build a German high seas fleet. I was busy at this time setting up the teaching of political and historical geography at the universities of Oxford and London, and was noting current events with a teacher's eye for generalisation. The German movement meant, I saw, that the nation already possessing the greatest organised land power and occupying the central strategical position in Europe was about to add to itself sea power strong enough to neutralise British sea power. The United States was also rising steadily to the rank of a Great Power. As yet, however, its rise could be measured only in statistical tables; although in my childhood someone had already been impressed with American resourcefulness, for I remember in our schoolroom a picture of the battle between the *Merrimac* and the *Monitor*, the first armoured ship and the first turret ship. Thus Germany and the United States came up alongside of Britain and Russia.

The particular events out of which sprang the idea of the Heartland were the British war in South Africa and the Russian war in Manchuria. The South African war ended in 1902, and in the spring of 1904 the Russo-Japanese war was clearly imminent. A paper which I read before the Royal Geographical Society early in the latter year, entitled *The Geographical Pivot of History*, was therefore topical, but it had a background of many years of observation and thought.

The contrast presented by the British war against the Boers, fought 6,000 miles away across the ocean, and the war fought by Russia at a comparable distance across the land expanse of Asia, naturally suggested a parallel contrast between Vasco da Gama rounding the Cape of Good Hope on his voyage to the Indies, near the end of the fifteenth century, and the ride of Yermak, the Cossack, at the head of his horsemen, over the Ural range into Siberia early in the sixteenth century. That comparison in turn led to a review of the long succession of raids made by the nomadic tribes of Central Asia, through classical antiquity and the Middle Ages, upon the settled populations of the crescent of subcontinents: peninsular Europe, the Middle East, the Indies, and China proper. My conclusion was that,

... in the present decade we are for the first time in a position to attempt, with some degree of completeness, a correlation between the larger geographical and the larger historical general-isations. For the first time we can perceive something of the real proportion of features and events on the stage of the whole world, and may seek a formula which shall express certain aspects, at any rate, of geographical causation in universal history. If we are fortunate, that formula should have a practical value as setting into perspective some of the competing forces in current international politics.

The word Heartland occurs once in the 1904 paper, but incidentally and as a descriptive and not a technical term. The expressions "pivot area" and "pivot state" were used instead, thus:

The oversetting of the balance of power in favor of the pivot state, resulting in its expansion over the marginal lands of Euro-Asia, would permit of the use of vast continental resources for fleet-building, and the empire of the world would then be in sight. This might happen if Germany were to ally herself with Russia.

In conclusion, it may be well expressly to point out that the substitution of some new control of the inland area for that of Russia would not tend to reduce the geographical significance of the pivot position. Were the Chinese, for instance, organised by the Japanese, to overthrow the Russian Empire and conquer its territory, they might constitute the yellow peril to the world's freedom just because they would add an oceanic frontage to the resources of the great continent.

At the end of the First World War, my book, *Democratic Ideals and Reality*, was published in London and New York.[5] Clearly the "pivot" label, which had been appropriate for an academic thesis at the beginning of the century, was no longer adequate to the international situation as it emerged from that first great crisis of our world revolution: hence "Ideals", "Realities" and the "Heartland." But the fact that, even when additional criteria were brought to bear, the thesis of 1904 still sufficed as the background for an estimate of the position fifteen years later, gave confidence that the formula sought had been found.

II

We turn now to the main object of the present article – the drafting of an interim estimate of the value of the Heartland concept in a survey of the world preliminary to the coming settlement. It must be understood that I am dealing with strategy, which, of course, is effective in peacetime no less than in wartime. I do not presume to join in the wide-sweeping debates already in progress which look forward over generations to come; I centre my thoughts on the years during which the enemy is to be held down while, in the language of Casablanca, his philosophy of war is being killed.

The Heartland is the northern part and the interior of Euro-Asia. It extends from the Arctic coast down to the central deserts, and has as its western limits the broad isthmus between the Baltic and Black Seas. The concept does not admit of precise definition on the map for the reason that it is based on three separate aspects of physical geography which, while reinforcing one another, are not exactly coincident. First of all, we have in this region by far the widest lowland plain on the face of the globe. Secondly, there flow across that plain some great navigable rivers; certain of them go north to the Arctic Sea and are inaccessible from the ocean because it is cumbered with ice, while others flow into inland waters, such as the Caspian, which have no exit to the ocean. Thirdly, there is here a grassland zone which, until within the last century and a half, presented ideal conditions for the development of high mobility by camel and horse-riding nomads. Of the three features mentioned, the river basins are the easiest to present cartographically; the water divide which delimits the whole group Arctic and "continental" rivers into a single unit does isolate neatly on the map a vast coherent area which is the Heartland according to that particular criterion. The mere exclusion of sea mobility and sea power, however, is a negative if important differential; it was the plain and the grassland belt which offered the positive conditions conducive to the other type of mobility, that proper to the prairie. As for the grassland, it traverses the whole breadth of the plain but does not cover its entire surface. Notwithstanding these apparent discrepancies, the Heartland provides a sufficient physical basis for strategical thinking. To go further and to simplify geography artificially would be misleading.

For our present purpose it is sufficiently accurate to say that the territory of the u.s.s.r. is equivalent to the Heartland, except in one direction. In order to demarcate that exception – a great one – let us draw a direct line, some 5,500 miles long, westward from Bering Strait to Rumania. Three thousand miles from Bering Strait that line will cross the Yenisei River, flowing north-ward from the borders of Mongolia to the Arctic Ocean. Eastward of that great river lies a generally rugged country of mountains, plateaux and valleys, covered almost from end to end with coniferous forests; this I shall call Lenaland, from its central feature, the great River Lena. This is not included in Heartland Russia. Lenaland Russia has an area of three and three-quarter million square miles, but a population of only some six millions, of whom almost five millions are settled along the transcontinental railroad from Irkutsk to Vladivostok. In the remainder of this territory there are on the average over three square miles for every inhabitant. The rich natural resources – timber, water power and minerals – are as yet practically untouched.

West of the Yenisei lies what I have described as Heartland Russia, a plain extending 2,500 miles north and south, and 2,500 miles east and west. It contains four and a quarter million square miles and a population of more than 170 millions.

The population is increasing at the rate of three millions a year.

The simplest and probably the most effective way of presenting the strategical values of the Russian Heartland is to compare them with those of France. In the case of France, however, the historical background is the First World War while in the case of Russia it is the Second World War.

France, like Russia, is a compact country, as long as it is broad, but not quite so well-rounded as the Heartland and therefore with a rather smaller area in proportion to the length of boundary to be defended. It is encompassed by sea and mountain, except to the northeast. In 1914-18 there were no hostile countries behind the Alps and the Pyrenees, and the fleets of France and her allies dominated the seas. The French and allied armies, deployed across the open northeastern frontier, were therefore well defended on either flank and were secure in the rear. The tragic lowland gateway in the northeast, through which so many armies have surged inward and outward, is 300 miles wide between the Vosges and the North Sea. In 1914, the line of battle, pivoting on the Vosges, wheeled backward to the Marne; and at the end of the war, in 1918, it wheeled forward on the same pivot. Through the four years' interval the elastic front sagged and bent but did not break even in the face of the great German attack in the spring of 1918. Thus, as it proved, there was space within the country sufficient both for defense in depth and for strategical retreat. Unfortunately for France, however, her principal industrial area was in that northeastern sector where the unceasing battle was waged.

Russia repeats in essentials the pattern of France, but on a greater scale and with her open frontier turned westward instead of northeastward. In the present war the Russian arm is aligned across that open frontier. In its rear is the vast plain of the Heartland, available for defense in depth and for strategic retreat. Away back, this plain recedes eastward into the natural bulwarks constituted by the "inaccessible" Arctic coast, the Lenaland wilderness behind the Yenisei, and the fringe of mountains from the Altai to the Hindu Kush, backed by the Gobi, Tibetan and Iranian deserts. These three barriers have breadth and substance, and far excel in defensive value the coasts and mountains which engird France.

It is true that the Arctic shore is no longer in-accessible in the absolute sense that held until a few years ago. Convoys of merchant ships, assisted by powerful icebreakers and with airplanes reconnoitring ahead for water lanes through the ice pack, have traded to the Obi and Yenisei Rivers, and even to the Lena River; but a hostile invasion across the vast area of circum-polar ice and over the Tundra mosses and Targa forests of Northern Siberia seems almost impossible in the face of Soviet land-based air defence.

To complete the comparison between France and Russia, let us consider the relative scales of some parallel facts. Heartland Russia has four times the population, four times as wide an open frontier, and twenty times the area of France. That open frontier is not disproportionate to the Russian population; and to equal the breadth of the Soviet deployment Germany has had to eke out her more limited manpower by diluting it with less effective troops drawn from her subject countries. In one important respect, however, Russia began her second war with Germany in no better position than France occupied in 1914; as with France, her most developed agriculture and industries lay directly in the path of the invader. The second Five Year Plan would have remedied that situation had the German aggression been delayed a couple of years. Perhaps that was one of Hitler's reasons for breaking his treaty with Stalin in 1941.

The vast potentialities of the Heartland, however, to say nothing of the natural reserves in Lenaland, are strategically well placed. Industries are growing rapidly in such localities as the southern Urals, in the very pivot of the pivot area, and in the rich Kuznetsk coal basin in the lee of the great natural barriers east of the upper Yenisei River. In 1938 Russia produced more of the following foodstuffs than any other country in the world: wheat, barley, oats, rye and sugar beets. More manganese was produced in Russia than in any other country. It was bracketed with the United States in the first place as regards iron, and it stood second place in production of petroleum. As for coal, Mikhaylov makes the statement that the resources of the Kuznetsk and Krasnoyarsk coal basins are each estimated to be capable of supplying the requirements of the whole world for 300 years.[6] The policy of the Soviet Government was to balance imports and exports during the first Five Year Plan. Except in a very few commodities the country is capable of producing everything which it requires.

All things considered, the conclusion is un-avoidable that if the Soviet Union emerges from this war as conqueror of Germany, she must rank as the greatest land Power on the globe. Moreover, she will be the Power in the strategically strongest defensive position. The Heartland is the greatest natural fortress on earth. For the first time in history it is manned by a garrison sufficient both in number and quality.

III

I cannot pretend to exhaust the subject of the Heartland, the citadel of land power on the great mainland of the world, in a short article like this. But a few words should be devoted to another concept to balance it.

From Casablanca there came lately the call to destroy the ruling German philosophy. That can be done only by irrigating the German mind with the clean water of a rival philosophy. I assume that for, say, two years from the time the "cease fire" order is given, the Allies will occupy Berlin, try the criminals, fix frontiers on the spot and complete other surgical treatment so that the older generation in Germany which will die impenitent and bitter cannot again misrepresent history to the younger generation. But it would obviously be worse than useless to set alien teachers to work in Germany to inculcate the theory of freedom. Freedom cannot be taught; it can only be given to those who can use it. However, the polluted channel might be swept clear very effectively if it were controlled by strong embankments of power on either hand – land power to the east, in the Heartland, and sea power to the west, in the North Atlantic basin. Face the German mind with an enduring certainty that any war fought by Germany must be a war on two *unshakable* fronts, and the Germans themselves will solve the problem.

For this to happen it will be necessary in the first place that there be effective and lasting cooperation between America, Britain and France, the first for depth of defense, the second as the moated forward stronghold – a Malta on a grander scale – and the third as the defensible bridgehead. The last is no less essential than the other two, because sea power must in the final resort be amphibious if it is to balance land power. In the second place, it is necessary that those three and the fourth conqueror, Russia, be pledged together to cooperate immediately if any breach of the peace is threatened, so that the devil in Germany can never again get its head up and must die by inanition.

Some persons today seem to dream of a global air power which will "liquidate" both fleets and armies.

I am impressed, however, by the broad implications of a recent utterance of a practical airman: "Air power depends absolutely on the efficiency of its ground organisation." That is too large a subject to discuss within the limits of this paper. It can only be said that no adequate proof has yet been presented that air fighting will not follow the long history of all kinds of warfare by presenting alternations of offensive and defensive tactical superiority, meanwhile effecting few permanent changes in strategical conditions.

I make no pretense to forecasting the future of humanity. What I am concerned with are the conditions under which we set about winning the peace when victory in the war has been achieved. In regard to the pattern of the postwar world, now being studied by many people for the first time, it is important that a line should be carefully drawn between idealistic blueprints and realistic and scholarly maps resenting concepts – political, economic, strategic, and so forth – based on the recognition of obstinate facts.

With that in mind, attention might be drawn to a great feature of global geography: a girdle, as it were, hung around the north polar regions. It begins as the Sahara desert, is followed as one moves eastward by the Arabian, Iranian, Tibetan and Mongolian deserts, and then extends, by way of the wildernesses of Lenaland, Alaska and the Laurentian shield of Canada, to the sub-arid belt of the western United States. That girdle of deserts and wildernesses is a feature of the first importance in global geography. Within it lie two related features of almost equal significance: the Heartland, and the basin of the Midland Ocean (North Atlantic) with its four subsidiaries (Mediterranean, Baltic, Arctic and Caribbean Seas). Outside the girdle is the Great Ocean (Pacific, Indian and South Atlantic) and the lands which drain to it (Asiatic Monsoon lands, Australia, South America and Africa south of the Sahara).

Archimedes said he could lift the world if he could find a fulcrum on which to rest his lever. All the world cannot be lifted back to prosperity at once. The region between the Missouri and the Yenisei, with its great trunk routes for merchant aircraft between Chicago-New York and London-Moscow, and all that the development of them will stand for, must be the first care, for it must be the fulcrum. Wisely the conquering of Japan waits for a while. In due course China will receive capital on a generous scale as a debt of honor, to help in her romantic adventure of building for a quarter of humanity a new civilisation, neither quite Eastern nor quite Western. Then the ordering of the Outer World will be relatively easy, with China, the United States and the United Kingdom leading the way, the last two each followed by its trail of a commonwealth of free nations – for though their histories will have been different the result will be similar. But the first enterprise undertaken in economic rebuilding will surely have to be in the area within the desert girdle, lest a whole civilisation should deliquesce into chaos. What a pity the alliance, negotiated after Versailles, between the United States, the United Kingdom and France was not implemented! What trouble and sadness that act might have saved!

IV

And now, to complete my picture of the pattern of the round world, let me add, briefly, three concepts to the two already visualised. For the purposes of what I see described in American writings as "Grand Strategy," it is necessary to build broad general-isations in geography no less than in history and economics.

I have described my concept of the Heartland, which I have no hesitation in saying is more valid and useful today than it was either twenty or forty years ago. I have said how it is set in its girdle of broad natural defenses – ice-clad Polar Sea, forested and rugged Lenaland, and Central Asiatic mountain and arid tableland. The girdle is incomplete, however, because of an open gateway, a thousand miles wide, admitting from Peninsular Europe into the interior plain through the broad isthmus between the Baltic and Black Seas. For the first time in all history there is within this vast natural fortress a garrison adequate to deny entry to the German invader. Given that fact, and the defenses to the flanks and rear which I have described, the sheer breadth of the open gateway is an advantage, for it provides the opportunity of defeating the enemy by compelling him to make a broad deployment of his manpower. And upon and beneath the Heartland there is a store of rich soil for cultivation and of ores and fuels for extraction, the equal – or thereabouts – of all that lies upon and beneath the United States and the Canadian Dominion.

I have suggested that a current of cleansing counter-philosophy, canalised between unbreachable embankments of power, may sweep the German mind clear of its black magic. Surely no one is going to be mad enough to set foreign teachers to exorcise the evil spirits from the soul of the conquered German nation. Nor, after the first inevitable punitory years, do I have sufficient trust that the conquering democracies will maintain garrisons of the necessary spirit and number *stationed in the vanquished lands*; for there is no use in asking democrats to persist in an attitude contrary to the very spirit and essence of democracy. The cleansing stream might better be released to flow from some regenerate and regenerating *German* source, between the embankments of power I have named, the one within the Heartland and the other within the territories of the three amphibious powers, American, British and French. The two friendly forces facing one another across the flow of the canal would be of equal power and should always be equally ready for necessary action. Then Germany would live continuously under the threat of immediate war on two fronts should she be guilty of any breach of the treaties which prohibited either physical preparation for war or the misleading of youth which is another way of preparation for war. The democratic garrisons in their home countries would be, by force of example, the teachers.

On this proposal follows my second geographical concept, that of the Midland Ocean – the North

Atlantic – and its dependent seas and river basins. Without labouring the details of that concept, let me picture it again in its three elements – a bridgehead in France, a moated aerodrome in Britain, and a reserve of trained manpower, agriculture and industries in the eastern United States and Canada. So far as war-potential goes, both the United States and Canada are Atlantic countries, and since instant land-warfare is in view, both the bridgehead and the moated aerodrome are essential to amphibious power.

The three remaining concepts I shall do little more than sketch, and only for the sake of globular completeness and balance. Girdling the twin unit just described – Heartland and the basin of the Midland Ocean – there appears on the globe the mantle of vacancies, constituting a practically continuous land-space covering some twelve million square miles – that is, about a quarter of all the land on the globe. Upon this vast area there lives today a total population of less than thirty millions, or, say, one-seventieth of the population of the globe. Airplanes will, of course, fly along many routes over this girdle of wilderness; and through it will be driven trunk motor roads. But for long to come it will break social continuity between the major communities of mankind on the globe.[7]

The fourth of my concepts embraces on either side of the South Atlantic the tropical rainforests of South America and Africa. If these were subdued to agriculture and inhabited with the present density of tropical Java, they might sustain a thousand million people, always provided that medicine had rendered the tropics as productive of human energy as the temperate zones.

Fifthly, and lastly, a thousand million people of ancient oriental civilisation inhabit the Monsoon lands of India and China. They must grow to prosperity in the same years in which Germany and Japan are being tamed to civilisation. They will then balance that other thousand million who live between the Missouri and the Yenisei. A balanced globe of human beings. And happy, because balanced and thus free.

NOTES

1. See *The Races of Europe*, by Prof. W. Z. RIPLEY (Kegan Paul, 1900).

2. This statement was criticised in the discussion which followed the reading of the paper. On reconsidering the paragraph, I still think it substantially correct. Even the Byzantine Greek would have been other than he was had Rome completed the subjugation of the ancient Greek. No doubt the ideals spoken of were Byzantine rather than Hellenic, but they were not Roman, which is the point.

3. It is not here intended that Nature has not changed in historic times, but only that the changes undergone by social Men have been vastly greater than the great changes of Nature in the same time. The mode of thought appropriate to this subject is that known in mathematics as the method of successive approximations.

4. Inertia, it must be remembered, implies not only difficulty in starting movement, but also difficulty in arresting or changing already existing movement.

5. A new edition, with text unaltered, was published last year by Henry Holt and Company, New York.

6. N. MIKHAYLOV, *Soviet Geography*, London: Methuen, 1937.

7. Some day, incidentally, when coal and oil are exhausted, the Sahara may become the trap for capturing direct power from the Sun.

DISCUSSION

On The Geographical Pivot of History

Below are the notes of Halford Mackinder's 1904 presentation of his paper The Geographical Pivot of History *at the Royal Geographical Society, recording the president's introduction and the discussion that took place between the audience and Mackinder after the talk.*

Before the reading of the paper, the PRESIDENT said: We are always very glad when we can induce our friend Mr. Mackinder to address us on any subject, because all he says to us is sure to be interesting and original and valuable. There is no necessity for me to introduce so old a friend of the Society to the meeting, and I will therefore at once ask him to read his paper.

• • •

After the reading of the paper, the PRESIDENT said: We hope that Mr. Spencer Wilkinson will offer some criticism on Mr. Mackinder's paper. Of course, it will not be possible to avoid geographical politics to a certain extent.

MR. SPENCER WILKINSON: It would occur to me that the most natural thing and the most sincere thing to say at the beginning is to endeavour to express the great gratitude which, I am sure, every one here feels for one of the most stimulating papers that has been read for a long time. As I was listening to the paper, I looked with regret on some of the space that is unoccupied here, and I much regret that a portion of it was not occupied by the members of the Cabinet, for I gathered that in Mr. Mackinder's paper we have two main doctrines laid down: the first, which is not altogether new – I think it was foreseen some years back in the last century – that since the modern improvements of steam navigation the whole of the world has become one, and has become one political system. I forget the exact expression that Mr. Mackinder used; I think he said that the difference was something like that of a shell falling into an enclosed structure and falling into space. I should wish to express the same thing by saying that, whereas only half a century ago statesmen played on a few squares of a chess-board of which the remainder was vacant, in the present day the world is an enclosed chess-board, and every movement of the statesman must take account of all the squares in it. I myself can only wish that we had ministers who would give more time to studying their policy from the point of view that you cannot move any one piece without considering all the squares on the board. We are very much too apt to look at our policy as though it were cut up into water-tight compartments, each of which had no connection with the rest of the world, whereas it seems to me the great fact of today is that any movement which is made in one part of the world affects the whole of the international relations of the world – a fact which, it seems to me, is lamentably neglected bath in British policy and in most of the popular discussions of it, and I am exceedingly grateful to Mr. Mackinder for having laid so much stress on that in his paper.

Then the other point – the main point, I take it, which he has brought out is really as to the enormous importance to the world of the modern expansion of Russia. I cannot say that I am thoroughly convinced of some of Mr. Mackinder's historical analogies or precedents, unless, indeed, we are to take his paper as carrying us a very long way ahead. Mr. Mackinder takes us back over four hundred years, and talks of the Columbian epoch. Well, I cannot pretend to be able to go four hundred years forward; if one can go a generation forward, it is quite as much as some of us can manage. Now, these great movements of Central Asian tribes on to Europe and on to the different marginal countries may, I think, be over-estimated in their importance. They have left occasional survivals of the past, but they have not left the world much richer in ideas, and very seldom represented any permanent alterations in the conditions of mankind; and they have been possible because the expanding forces of Central Asia hit upon a very much divided margin. For instance, the movement of the Ottoman Turks, and before that the Turkish movements upon the Byzantine Empire and upon the region that had been the Byzantine Empire, invariably struck upon regions in which government was in decay or obsolescent, and most of the movements which struck upon Central Europe, the movements north of the Black sea, struck upon Europe at a time when government was very little organised, and when the states had very little of solidarity between them.

Therefore, I hold they do not afford very much parallel for the future; and I should be disposed to dwell on the counter-balancing phenomenon, which is that you have had in the west of Europe a small island, which, having attained to its own political unity, and having in the conflict for its own independence developed its sea-power, has been able to affect the marginal regions and to acquire the enormous influence which was revealed to us, a little exaggerated, perhaps, on the map which Mr. Mackinder showed – the British Empire – exaggerated because it was a map on Mercator's projection, which exaggerated the British Empire, with the exception of India. My own belief is that an island state like our own can, if it maintains its naval power, hold the balance between the divided forces which work on the continental area, and I believe that has been the historical function of Great Britain since Great Britain was a United Kingdom. Now we find a smaller island state rising on the opposite side of the Euro-Asian continent, and I see no reason at all to suppose that that state should not be able to exercise on the eastern fringe of the Asiatic continent a power as decisive and as influential as that which the British Isles, with a smaller population, have exercised upon Europe.

SIR THOMAS HOLDICH: When one hears a lecture such as Mr. Mackinder has just given us, so full of thought and so thoroughly well worked out, with such an amount of food for reflection contained in it, it takes a great deal of moral digestion to assimilate it, and more assurance than I possess either to criticise it, or even to discuss it. But there is just one question I should like to ask Mr. Mackinder, and in co-relating the facts of geographical conditions with the history of the human race, it seems to me a not unimportant one. Mr. Mackinder has told us that in the beginning of things the Mongol races all started from a centre in high Asia, spreading outwards, westwards, southwards, and eastwards, finding, however, Tibet an impossible barrier in their way, and never exactly occupying India. But we must remember that before the Mongolians spread, there were other Central Asian tribes who spread equally from districts which were not so very far removed from the position which the Mongolians themselves first occupied – the Scyths and the Aryans – and that they did find their way into India. That, however, is a matter of detail.

What I should like to know from Mr. Mackinder is, what he considers to be the original reason of that extraordinary overflow from the country which we are disposed to consider to be the cradle of the human race, to all the different parts of the world. Was it simply the nomadic instincts of the people, a sort of hereditary compulsion which obliged them to flow outwards; or was it an actual alteration in the physical characteristics of the country in which they dwelt? We know that the physical conditions of the world alter very much from time to time, and it seems to me impossible to reconcile the idea of a great inland country, which must once have been full of a teeming population, and have supported that population, as you may say, with an abundant power of agricultural wealth – that under such conditions a people should have had a desire to spread out and to wander forth into other parts of the world, seeking for they knew not what. I fancy, myself, that one of the great reasons, one of the great compelling reasons, for all these migrations really has been a distinct alteration in the physical condition of the country. That is a point which seems to me to be rather important when we are discussing a subject like the present one, which brings the 'conditions of geography to bear on the facts of history.

There is just one other little matter which was referred to somewhat doubtfully by Mr. Mackinder to which I might refer. He pointed to South America as a possible factor in that outer belt of power which was to bring coercion to bear on the inner power pivoting about the south of Russia. Now, from what I have seen lately, I have not the least doubt that that will be the case. The potentiality of South America as a naval power I look upon as very great. I believe that in the course, say, of the next half-century, in spite of the fact that just now Argentina has sold two ships to Japan, and Chili has sold a couple of ships to us – in spite of that fact, there will be an increase of naval strength in South America, resulting from purely natural causes, for the defence of her own coast and the protection of her own traffic, which will be only comparable to the extraordinary development which we have seen during the last half-century in Japan. This seems to me certainly to be one of the factors, if we are to look forward, with which, in the future naval politics of the world, we shall have to reckon.

Mr. Amery: I think it is always enormously interesting if we can occasionally get away from the details of everyday politics and try to see things as a whole, and this is what Mr. Mackinder's most stimulating lecture has done for us tonight. He has given us the whole of history and the whole of ordinary politics under one big comprehensive idea. I remember when I did Herodotus at the university, he made the whole of history base itself upon the great struggle between the east and the west. Mr. Mackinder makes the whole of history and politics base themselves on the great economical struggle between the great inside core of the Euro-Asiatic continent and the smaller marginal regions and islands outside. I am not sure myself that these two struggles are not one and the same, because now we have discovered that the world is a sphere, east and west have only become relative terms. I would criticise one thing Mr. Mackinder said when he described Russia as the heir of Greece. It was not the ancient heir of Hellenic Greece, but of Byzantium, and Byzantium was the heir of the old Oriental monarchies with the Greek language and a tinge of Roman civilisation thrown over it. I should like to go back, if I might, for a moment to this geographical economic foundation on which Mr. Mackinder built the framework of his lecture.

I think I would conceive the thing somewhat differently. There are, to my mind, not two, but three economico-military forces. If we begin with the ancient world, you have the broad geographical division into the "steppes" of the interior, the rich marginal land suitable for agriculture, and the coast, and you have corresponding with these, three economical and three military systems. There is the economical and military system of the agricultural country, the system of the coast and sea-faring people, and the system of the steppes; each had its peculiar weaknesses and its peculiar sources of strength. The strongest in many ways was the marginal and agricultural state. There you got the great solid military Empires, your Egyptian, your Babylonian, your Roman Empire, your large armies and citizen infantry, your great development of wealth.

But these contained certain elements of weakness. Their own prosperity or the defects of their form of government would lead ultimately to slothfulness and weakness. Now, outside those you had two other systems. You had the steppe system, whose military strength lay, firstly, in its mobility, and, secondly, in its inaccessibility from the slower-moving agricultural powers. As regards the supposed "hordes" of invaders which came from the interior, I do not myself believe there ever were those very large hordes and large populations in the interior. The fact is this, the steppe populations were small then as now, but from the fact of their mobility the heavier and slower military armies could not successfully attack them. In ordinary times, when the agricultural states were strong, the people of the steppes simply ran away from them, and the others found it too much trouble to conquer them. You remember the difficulty the Roman legions had with the Parthians; and I think we can find a very much more recent example of the difficulty a civilised state finds in conquering a steppe-power. Only a short time ago, the whole of the British army was occupied in trying to coerce some 40,000 or 50,000 farmers who lived on a dry steppe-land. That photograph Mr. Mackinder was showing reminded me

97

exactly of what you could have seen not so many months ago in South Africa – I mean, that picture of waggons crossing the river was, except for the shape of the roof over the waggon, exactly like a picture of a Boer commando crossing a drift. We had the same difficulty in coercing them that all civilised powers have had with steppe people. Now, whenever the civilised powers on the marginal countries have grown weak and have allowed small hired armies to do their work, they have got into difficulties, and that is where, it seems to me, the strength of the steppes has always come in. There is no great economic strength at bottom, but the fact that they could retire into their inaccessible wilderness, and come upon the others in times of their weakness, gave the steppe peoples their power. Then there is the third system, that of the maritime coast peoples: they had even less pure military strength, but they had the greatest mobility – the mobility, I mean, of the Vikings or the Saracens when they ruled the Mediterranean, and the Elizabethan Englishmen when they harried the Spanish Main. Coming to more modern times, there has been a certain further change in the agricultural conditions, and the development, out of the old agricultural states, of the modern industrial state.

Then I would also notice that many countries which were steppe became agricultural and industrial. You have that, and you have also the fact that very rarely in history do you get any state rising to great power by one system alone. The Turks began by being the people of the steppes, and came down and swept over Asia Minor; they then formed a regular military power, and conquered the great Turkish Empire; lastly, for a period they became the leading naval power in the Mediterranean. In the same way, you find the Romans, in order to beat the Carthaginians, became a sea-power as well as a land-power; and, in fact, for a power to be great it must have both these elements of strength. The Romans were a great military power with the marginal region as their base and with sea-power behind them. We ourselves have always had as a base the industrial wealth of England. The Russian Empire, which covers the great steppe region, but is no longer in the hands of the old steppe people, is really a portion of the agricultural world, economically, which has conquered the steppe and is turning it into a great agricultural industrial power, and therefore giving a power which the pure steppe people never possessed.

Mr. Mackinder referred to the fact that it is only within the last century that the agricultural races have occupied and populated the southern steppe of Russia proper. They are doing the same thing in Central Asia; in fact, the old steppe people are being squeezed out altogether, and you get, coming closer and closer together, two leading industrial-military powers, the one radiating out from a continental centre, and the other beginning from the sea, but gradually going further into the continent in order to have the big industrial base which it requires, because sea-power alone, if it is not based on great industry, and has a great population behind it, is too weak for offence to really maintain itself in the world struggle. I do not intend to make many more remarks, but there is just one point – a word of Mr. Mackinder's suggested it to me. Horse and camel mobility has largely passed away; and it is now a question of railway-mobility as against sea-mobility. I should like to say that sea-mobility has gained enormously in military strength to what it was in ancient times, especially in the number of men that can be carried.

In the old days the ships were mobile enough, but they carried few men, and the raids of the sea-people were comparatively feeble. I am not suggesting anything political at the present time; I am merely stating a fact when I say that the sea is far better for conveying troops than anything, except fifteen or twenty parallel lines of railway. What I was coming to is this: that both the sea and the railway are going in the future – it may be near, or it may be somewhat remote – to be supplemented by the air as a means of locomotion, and when we come to that (as we are talking in broad Columbian epochs, I think I may be allowed to look forward a bit) – when we come to that, a great deal of this geographical distribution must lose its importance, and the successful powers will be those who have the greatest industrial basis. It will not matter whether they are in the centre of a continent or on an island; those people who have the industrial power and the power of invention and of science will be able to defeat all others. I will leave that as a parting suggestion.

MR. HOGARTH: As the hour is rather late and the temperature rather low, I will not take up your time with any very lengthy remarks. We certainly have had a wonderfully suggestive paper, and I think it is neither necessary to advise the reader of the paper nor any one who has listened to it to try and think imperially. I would only ask Mr. Mackinder, when he replies, to make me certain about one point. Does he really mean to imply – I think it is an interesting fact if be meant to establish it – that the state of things which is coming to pass in this inner pivot land will be entirely different to anything that has been seen there before? That is to say, something like a stationary state of things has been brought about, and the country is being developed, till it will even be able to export its own products to the rest of the world; and therefore we are never to see again the state of things that has existed all through ancient history in that a great central region which has continually sent its populations down into the marginal countries, while the marginal countries have sent back to it their influences of civilisation, each operating in turn upon the other. The only other observation I would like to make is to reinforce Mr. Amery's objection to Mr. Mackinder's Graeco-Slav. I am afraid I cannot accept that division of civilisation between the Greek and the Roman. So far as Russia can be called a civilised country at this moment, it has, I think, not been civilised by the Orthodox Church ; in fact, I have yet to learn of any civilising influence exerted by the Orthodox Church on a great scale. Its civilisation is far more due to the social culture which was introduced by Peter the Great, and that was more Roman than Greek.

But it is to my first question I should like Mr. Mackinder to give a clear answer. I should like to know what he seriously anticipates is going to be the effect on the world of this new distinction between the marginal and the central pivot lands.

MR. MACKINDER: I have to thank all the speakers for dotting my i's and crossing my t's. I am delighted to find my formula work so well. I do mean exactly what Mr. Hogarth says; I mean that for the first time within recorded history – and this is in reply to Sir Thomas Holdich as well – you have a great stationary population being developed in the steppe lands. This is a revolution in the world that we have to face and reckon with. I doubt very much, and there I agree with Mr. Amery, whether the numbers who came from the heart of Asia were very great. It seems to me quite as he puts it, and that their mobility was of the very essence of the whole thing. A small number of people coming from the steppe lands could do many things, given relative mobility as compared with the agricultural population. With regard to Sir Thomas Holdich's inquiry as to what should send them forth, Sir Clements Markham has pointed out that the nomads did not pour forth once only. I dealt with the fact that for a thousand years the nomadic peoples came through Russia. I fail to see that, when you have this constant succession of descents upon the marginal lands, you are called upon to ask for any special physical change to explain it. All the accounts we have from the time of the earliest Greeks describe the drinkers of mares' milk, and picture for us the nomadic mode of life; therefore I start with the fact that these peoples were nomadic and remained nomadic through two thousand years, and I do not see any evidence that we need either to call in any great physical change or yet to assume any great settled population.

As far as I can see, Sven Hedin refuses the idea that you must necessarily ask for a great change of climate in order to explain the existence of the remains in Central Asia. You have powerful winds and much sand, and from time to time the sand is swept over hundreds of miles across the desert. The sand determines the flow of the rivers and the position of the lakes, and some great storm diverting a river into another course would no doubt suffice to ruin a town abandoned by the water. The mere fact that there were nomads, and that there were rich countries to be plundered, seems to me to be almost sufficient for my theory. In the future, I think, you are bound to have different economic provinces, one based mainly on the sea, and the other on the heart of the continent and on railways.

I do not think Mr. Amery has allowed sufficiently for the fact that the very largest armies cannot be moved by means of a navy. The Germans marched nearly a million men into France; they marched, and used the railways for supplies. Russia, by her tariff system and in other ways, is steadily hastening the accomplishment of what I may call the non-oceanic economic system. Her whole policy, by her tariff system, by her break of gauge on her railways, is to separate herself from external oceanic competition. With regard to the basis of sea-power in industrial wealth, I absolutely agree.

What I suggest is that great industrial wealth in Siberia and European Russia and a conquest of some of the marginal regions would give the basis for a fleet necessary to found the world empire. Mr. Amery's way of putting the three groups of powers is slightly different from mine, but it is essentially the same. I ask for an inner land mobility, for a margin densely populated, and for external sea forces. It is true the camel-men and the horse-men are going; but my suggestion is that railways will take their place, and then you will be able to fling power from side to side of this area. My aim is not to predict a great future for this or that country, but to make a geographical formula into which you could fit any political balance.

There was a point with regard to the Graeco-Slav: in the sense in which Mr. Hogarth and Mr. Amery have taken me, I agree with them, but after all I cannot help feeling that Christianity fell on two very different soils – the Greek philosophic and the Roman legal, and that it has in consequence differently influenced the Slav and the Teuton. However, that is a mere incident, and if I qualify my statement by speaking of the Byzantine, I shall then get near to what Mr. Amery asks; and I think I shall do away with the necessity of introducing the example of Rome which Mr. Hogarth brought forward. As regards the potentialities of the land and of the people, I would point out that in Europe there are now more than 40,000,000 people in the steppe land of Russia, and it is by no means yet densely occupied, and that the Russian population is probably increasing faster than any other great civilised or half-civilised population in the world. With a decreasing French population, and a British not increasing as fast as it was, and the native-born populations of the United States and Australia coming nearly to a standstill, you have to face the fact that in a hundred years 40,000,000 people have occupied but a mere corner of the steppe. I think you are on the way to a population which will be numbered by the hundred million; and this is a tendency which you must take into account in assigning values to the variable quantities in the equation of power for which I was seeking a geographical formula. The point with regard to Korea and the Persian gulf which was put by Mr. Spencer Wilkinson exactly illustrates my correlation of the Far Eastern, Middle Eastern, and Near Eastern questions.

I represent these as being the present temporary form of the collision between the external and internal forces acting through the intermediate zone, which is itself the seat of independent forces. I quite agree that the function of Britain and of Japan is to act upon the marginal region, maintaining the balance of power there as against the expansive internal forces. I believe that the future of the world depends on the maintenance of this balance of power. It appears to me that our formula makes it clear that we must see to it that we are not driven out of the marginal region. We must maintain our position there, and then, whatever happens, we are fairly secure. The increase of population in the inner regions and the stoppage of increase in the outer regions may be rather serious; but perhaps South America will come in to help us.

The PRESIDENT: I confess I have been entranced by Mr. Mackinder's paper, and I could see by the close attention with which it was listened to by the audience that you all shared my feeling in that respect.

Mr. Mackinder has dealt with the old, old story from the very dawn of history, the struggle between Ormerzd and Ahriman, and he has shown us how that struggle has continued on from the very dawn of history to the present day.

He has explained all this to us with a brilliancy of description and of illustration, with a close grasp of the subject, and with a clearness of argument which we have seldom had equalled in this room. I am sure you will all with me give a unanimous vote of thanks to Mr. Mackinder for his most interesting paper this evening.

PUBLICATION SOURCES

The Geographical Pivot of History

Read at the Royal Geographical Society, 25 January 1904. First published in *The Geographical Journal*, Vol. 23, No. 4 (April 1904), pp. 421-437.

The Physical Basis of Political Geography

Presented at a meeting of the Royal Scottish Geographical Society, Edinburgh, 18 December 1889. First published in *Scottish Geographical Magazine*, Vol. 6, No. 2 (February 1890), pp. 78-84.

The Round World and the Winning of the Peace

First published in *Foreign Affairs*, Vol. 21, No. 4 (July 1943), pp. 595-605. Reproduced with permission of the Council on Foreign Relations.